# THE SOUTHERN HUMANITIES CONFERENCE
# AND ITS CONSTITUENT SOCIETIES

# THE SOUTHERN HUMANITIES CONFERENCE AND ITS CONSTITUENT SOCIETIES

COMPILED BY

J. O. BAILEY

AND

STURGIS E. LEAVITT

Bulletin Number Two
The Southern Humanities Conference

THE UNIVERSITY OF NORTH CAROLINA PRESS

1951

## PREFACE

With this Bulletin the Southern Humanities Conference continues its efforts in behalf of humanistic scholarship in the South. By giving publicity to the history of the Conference and its constituent societies, it is hoped that the aims of the association will be better known and that moral, and even financial, support in the South will be forthcoming. It seems only logical for the intellectual South to keep pace with the industrial South.

The Southern Humanities Conference is feeling its way toward giving aid and comfort to the Humanities in its territory. It will welcome any suggestions leading to the development of interest in a field which is of particular concern to this region.

The compilers of this Bulletin gratefully acknowledge the assistance of the secretaries and representatives of the constituent societies of the Southern Humanities Conference in supplying information about the history of these associations.

J. O. BAILEY<br>
STURGIS E. LEAVITT

# CONTENTS

| | PAGE |
|---|---|
| Preface | v |

### THE SOUTHERN HUMANITIES CONFERENCE

| | |
|---|---|
| History | 1 |
| Meetings and Officers | 25 |

### HISTORIES OF THE CONSTITUENT SOCIETIES

| | |
|---|---|
| American Musicological Society, Southeastern Chapter | 37 |
| Classical Association of the Middle West and South, Southern Section | 38 |
| College Art Association, Southeastern Regional Conference | 41 |
| Society of Biblical Literature and Exegesis, Southern Section | 43 |
| South Atlantic Modern Language Association | 44 |
| South-Central Modern Language Association | 47 |
| Southeastern Library Association | 48 |
| Southern Historical Association | 51 |
| Southern Society for the Philosophy of Religion | 55 |
| Southern Society for Philosophy and Psychology | 56 |

### THE SOUTHERN HUMANITIES CONFERENCE

| | |
|---|---|
| Associate Members | 61 |
| Constitution | 63 |

THE SOUTHERN HUMANITIES CONFERENCE

# HISTORY

The Old South is a memory and a legend. Historians may see what was one-sided in the plantation economy, but the memory and the legend bear testimony to a gracious and cultured life in a fruitful land. This gracious life fostered an ideal of great men—Washington, Jefferson, Calhoun, Lanier, Lee—and sought to develop the ideal in colleges like William and Mary and in our earliest state universities, such as North Carolina, Georgia, and Virginia. The New South of the present century seems to have lost, in some degree, this ideal of human greatness and to have given emphasis to more material things. Industries stretch from the Valley of Virginia through the TVA region and to the oil fields of Texas. The new order fosters the ideal of wealth and general welfare, and it gives support to popular education. Colleges and universities flourish in the South, but they are growing larger and prouder in devotion to commerce, technological skills, and professional training. If one could judge from current advertisements alone, the New South might be looked upon as a Promised Land of the Philistines.

But not entirely so. The new prosperity may, in some measure, be the basis for a renaissance. Cultural activities in behalf of scholarship, research, and publication find support in vigorous and rapidly growing organizations of scholars and teachers—in languages and literatures, in music, art, library work, history, philosophy, and religion. If the impulses to promote the humanities found in these organizations could be coordinated, a step might be taken toward that renaissance, toward a union of ideals in an economically abundant and yet gracious and cultured life.

The Southern Humanities Conference is an effort to promote research in the humanities through coordination of efforts already being made. The idea for the Conference originated in many minds. When one person spoke of it, others developed its possibilities from their own previous thought. For example, after a Committee of the American Council of Learned Societies was formed on the Pacific Coast and when it decided to explore the status of the humanities and the research being done in that region, Thomas B. Stroup, Chairman of the Committee on the Humanities of the South Atlantic Modern Language Association, talked with Sturgis E. Leavitt, Editor of the *South Atlantic Bulletin* and member of the Board of Directors of the American Council of Learned Societies, about the possibility of a similar survey in the South. Mr. Stroup found that Waldo G. Leland of the American Council had discussed with Mr. Leavitt the formation of a committee in the South. Mr. Leavitt already had in mind the sending of a letter on this topic to the officers of Southern groups and editors of Southern journals concerned with the humanities.

Exactly in whose mind the idea of an All-Southern Committee on the Humanities originated is not crystal clear, but all the evidence points to the fertile brain of Waldo G. Leland, then Director of the American Council of Learned Societies.

\* \* \*

The next step is a matter of official record. In October, 1944, the letter mentioned above was mailed to the officers of a conference on the Humanities held at Vanderbilt University in July of that year, to the Southern Association of Colleges and Secondary Schools, the Classical Association of the Middle West and South, the South Atlantic Modern Language Association, the South-Central Modern Language Association, the Southern Society for Philosophy and Psychology, and to the editors of the *Sewanee Review,* the *South Atlantic Quarterly,* the *William and Mary Quarterly,* the *Virginia Quarterly,* and the *North Carolina Historical Review.*

The letter asked for opinions regarding the value of a conference to be held in the spring of 1945 "to discuss practical aspects of the Humanities in the South." The topics suggested for this conference included "A United Front for Humanities in the South," "Formation of a Southern Council for the Humanities," and other "valuable contacts" among the associations. Replies were generally favorable to the conference. Walter Clyde Curry of Vanderbilt University wrote that the proposed conference "would go far in furthering the objectives" of the Vanderbilt Conference; Fletcher M. Green wrote, for the Southern Historical Association, that "discussion might open up possibilities" for the various groups to "cooperate in the furtherance of their common interests." Walter R. Agard wrote, for the Classical Association of the Middle West and South, that his association "would like to be represented in the conference"; G. R. Vowles wrote, for the South Atlantic Modern Language Association, that a conference to "assure a lively exchange of opinion" would be "highly worthwhile." The idea, then, seemed to be a good one, but just what the conference might, or could, do was not as yet apparent.

These expressions were reported to the American Council of Learned Societies. The American Council was interested, but because wartime travel was difficult and since it was thought that the Vanderbilt Conference might hold periodical meetings, the Council decided to delay action.

\* \* \*

The war came to an end, and the Vanderbilt Conference did not continue meeting. In February, 1947, therefore, Mr. Leavitt again communicated with leaders in the South regarding the advisability of holding a conference and perhaps forming a "Regional Committee on the Humanities." Among topics for discussion, he proposed the question whether various societies might "work together to promote the cause of the Humanities in the South (a) by encouraging cooperation of departments within institutions, (b) by the early discovery of promising young scholars, (c) by the promotion of graduate study, (d) by encouragement of research, and (e) by library cooperation."

Replies to this letter were so encouraging that plans were made to hold the conference without further delay. The American Council of Learned Societies cooperated fully, and Richard H. Shryock, Acting Director of the Council, issued an invitation on April 15, stating: "At the suggestion of some of the officers of the South Atlantic Modern Language Association, the Council is sponsoring an exploratory conference to be held in Chapel Hill, North Carolina, on May 17-18, 1947, with a view to the possible establishment of a Regional Committee on the Humanities."

The meeting was held, and the following representatives of Southern societies attended: Allan H. Gilbert, President, and Thomas B. Stroup,[1] of the South Atlantic Modern Language Association; Arthur H. Moser, President, and B. L. Ullman, representing the Classical Association of the Middle West and South, Southern Section; B. v. H. Gilmer, President, and Joseph Weitz, Secretary, of the Southern Society for Philosophy and Psychology; T. D. Clark, President, and James W. Patton, Secretary, of the Southern Historical Association; George Pope Shannon, representing the Work Conference on Higher Education of the Southern Association of Colleges and Secondary Schools; Louis R. Wilson, repre-

---

[1] Chairman of the Committee on the Humanities, a fact stated above. Hereafter to avoid repetition, a person's position and affiliation are stated the first time his name is mentioned, but not repeated.

senting the Southeastern Library Association; and Kenneth W. Clark, representing the Society of Biblical Literature and Exegesis. Besides these representatives of societies, the following were present as advisers: Hardin Craig (English, University of North Carolina); Glen Haydon (Music, University of North Carolina); A. P. Hudson (English, University of North Carolina); Jay B. Hubbell (English, Duke University); Louis O. Kattsoff (Philosophy, University of North Carolina); Charles S. Sydnor (History, Duke University); and Richard H. Shryock. Members of the local committee on arrangements were J. O. Bailey (English, University of North Carolina); Loren C. MacKinney (History, University of North Carolina); and Sturgis E. Leavitt (Spanish, University of North Carolina), Chairman.

When the meeting convened, the following temporary officers were elected: Mr. Leavitt, Chairman, and Mr. Bailey, Secretary. The Chairman introduced Mr. Shryock, who explained that the purpose of the American Council in calling the conference was to consider the formation of a permanent committee to engage in cooperative work for the promotion of humane learning in the South. He suggested that delegates of each Southern society might be selected for this committee; the committee might be autonomous, but might expect encouragement and to some extent financial support from the American Council of Learned Societies. Representatives of the societies each spoke of the interest of his society in the general problems of the humanities. Each expressed a favorable attitude toward the proposed committee and willingness to convey recommendations to his society.

The Chairman then asked the question: "What is to be done through a permanent Southern Committee on the Humanities?" Various answers were given. Through the committee, the societies might engage in joint undertakings, provide one another with information about their activities, survey research in progress in the South in all humanistic fields and publish the results, survey resources for the advanced study of Southern culture, and provide general encouragement of scholarship in the South. It was suggested that, looking toward widespread coordination, an index of Southern societies concerned with the humanities might be prepared. A survey of research in progress in the South was considered a desirable joint undertaking. The group considered it desirable to publish news about the Humanities and the activities of the various societies and their members.

The group then formed itself into a temporary Southern Regional Committee on the Humanities, and a sub-committee was appointed to prepare recommendations for a constitution. Mr. Shryock stated his willingness to recommend to the American Council that it assume the financial burden of bringing the group together again to hear the reports of exploratory sub-committees. It was decided that this meeting should be held in October, 1947, and the meeting adjourned.

\* \* \*

James W. Patton, Kenneth W. Clark, and B. L. Ullman, with Sturgis E. Leavitt, as Chairman of the Conference, and J. O. Bailey, Secretary, *ex officiis,* met in Chapel Hill on June 17 as a committee on arrangements for the next meeting. On the invitation of Mr. Clark, it was decided to hold the October conference at Duke University.

The second meeting of the group to form the Southern Humanities Council (the name then selected) convened at Duke University on October 25, 1947, to hear reports from the committees, to perfect plans for a permanent organization, and to adopt a constitution. The following were present:

## History

Sturgis E. Leavitt, Chairman *pro tem;* J. O. Bailey, Secretary, *pro tem.;* Cornelius Krusé, Executive Director of the American Council of Learned Societies; Albert G. A. Balz (Philosophy, University of Virginia), representing the Southern Society for Philosophy and Psychology; Kenneth W. Clark; T. D. Clark; Hardin Craig; Allan H. Gilbert; B. v. H. Gilmer; Glen Haydon; Jay B. Hubbell; Arthur P. Hudson; L. O. Kattsoff; Loren C. MacKinney; Arthur H. Moser; Roscoe E. Parker (English, University of Tennessee), representing the Southern Association of Colleges and Secondary Schools; James W. Patton, Thomas B. Stroup, and B. L. Ullman.

Mr. Leavitt surveyed the history of the efforts to form the Southern Humanities Council and welcomed Mr. Krusé as the representative of the American Council of Learned Societies. Mr. Krusé, discussing the relation between the American Council and the Southern Humanities Council stated that, acting with initiative and a large measure of autonomy, the Southern Council might at the same time serve as a committee through which the American Council might make effective impact upon the life of the South. He suggested that the Southern Council should plan projects that were sound, imaginative, and wisely conceived, and then seek support for them from Southern foundations.

Mr. Parker spoke of the relationship between the Southern Humanities Council and the Southern Association of Colleges and Secondary Schools. Recognizing the intention of the Council to invite the Southern Association to become a member-organization, he was uncertain whether the Southern Association could become a member. As the two organizations were parallel, both covering various interests and representing various societies, he suggested coordination, rather than membership.

The group then turned to consideration of the proposed constitution. It provided that the Southern Humanities Council invite the following organizations to become members:

>South Atlantic Modern Language Association
>South-Central Modern Language Association
>Southern Association of Colleges and Secondary Schools
>Southern Section of the Classical Association of the Middle West and South
>Southeastern Chapter, American Musicological Society
>Southeastern Conference of the College Art Association
>Southeastern Library Association
>Southern Historical Association
>Southern Society for Philosophy and Psychology
>Southern Society for the Philosophy of Religion

It provided for the admission of other organizations devoted to humanistic studies in the South, for four members-at-large, and for representation from the American Council of Learned Societies. Upon adoption of the constitution, it was decided to issue invitations to the various organizations to become members and appoint delegates.

Mr. Stroup reported steps he was taking to make a survey of research in the Humanities in the South; Mr. Bailey reported progress in preparing an index of Southern societies in the fields of the Humanities. Mr. Stroup reported the activities of Herman Spivey (then of the University of Florida) in making a survey of resources for advanced study in the South. The Council voted to authorize Mr. Spivey to continue this work under the auspices of the Council. Mr. Balz proposed completion and publication, partly with the support of the Council, of a survey of teaching and teachers of philosophy in the South, the survey to be partly biographical and partly bibliographical.

In January, 1948, the American Council of Learned Societies

voted to continue support of the group, but expressed the desire that it change its name to Southern Humanities Conference, to avoid confusion with the national organization.

The delegates chosen by the constituent organizations proceeded to elect by mail-ballot four members-at-large: J. O. Bailey, W. C. Binkley (History, Vanderbilt University), Thomas H. English (English, Emory University), and B. L. Ullman.

\* \* \*

The third meeting of the group, and the first as the officially constituted Southern Humanities Conference, was held in Chapel Hill on April 23-24, 1948. Delegates of the Southern societies attending the Conference were: Albert G. A. Balz, Southern Society for Philosophy and Psychology; Fletcher M. Green (History, University of North Carolina, alternate for T. D. Clark), Southern Historical Association; Glen Haydon, Southeastern Chapter of the American Musicological Association; Ernest E. Leisy (English, Southern Methodist University, alternate for Allan D. McKillop of Rice Institute), South Central Modern Language Association; Arthur H. Moser, Southern Section of the Classical Association of the Middle West and South; R. L. Patterson (Philosophy, Duke University), Southern Society for Philosophy of Religion; Thomas B. Stroup, South Atlantic Modern Language Association; Clemens Sommer (Art, University of North Carolina), Southeastern Conference of the College Art Association; and Louis R. Wilson, Southeastern Library Association. Members-at-large attending the meeting were: J. O. Bailey, Thomas H. English, and B. L. Ullman. Sturgis E. Leavitt attended as representative of the American Council of Learned Societies; Roscoe E. Parker, as observer for the Southern Association of Colleges and Secondary Schools.

The Chairman presented an application of the Southern Section of the Society of Biblical Literature and Exegesis for membership in the Southern Humanities Conference. This organization was admitted to membership, and its delegate, Kenneth W. Clark, was welcomed to the Conference.

In accordance with the constitutional provision for rotation of delegates and members-at-large, terms of membership were chosen by lot, as follows: for 1948-1949, delegates of the South Central Modern Language Association, the Southeastern Library Association, and the Southern Section of the Society of Biblical Literature and Exegesis; for 1948-1950, delegates of the South Atlantic Modern Language Association, the Southeastern Conference of the College Art Association, and the Southeastern Chapter of the American Musicological Society; for 1948-1951, delegates of the Southern Society for Philosophy and Psychology, the Southern Section of the Classical Association of the Middle West and South, the Southern Historical Association, and the Southern Society for Philosophy of Religion. Membership of members-at-large was determined to be: 1948-1949, J. O. Bailey; 1948-1950, B. L. Ullman; and 1948-1951, Thomas H. English and W. C. Binkley. The term of Mr. Leavitt, representing the American Council of Learned Societies, was left to the decision of the American Council.

Mr. Leavitt, Chairman *pro tem.*, and Mr. Bailey, Secretary *pro tem.*, were continued as Chairman and Secretary through the coming year.

Mr. Stroup presented the report of his committee on research in progress in the South. Aided by Rembert Patrick (University of Florida, representing the Southern Historical Association), Arthur Moore (Tulane, representing the South Central Modern Language Association), Albert G. A. Balz, and

Miss Carolyn E. Bock (Northwestern State College, Louisiana, representing the Southern Section of the Classical Association of the Middle West and South) the committee had sent letters of inquiry to scholars in every institution in the South; replies were being organized and edited. Mr. Stroup proposed listing, by author and by subject-matter, all research in progress, including dissertations, in Maryland, the District of Columbia, Virginia, Kentucky, North Carolina, Tennessee, Arkansas, Oklahoma, Texas, Louisiana, Mississippi, Alabama, Georgia, South Carolina, and Florida. The present data indicated about one thousand research-scholars active in the South on about fifteen hundred research-projects ranging from an encyclopedia of Greek and Roman foods to an analysis of current events.

Mr. Stroup described the work being done by Herman Spivey's Committee on Americana of the South Atlantic Modern Language Association on a Guide to Southern Manuscript Resources. Mr. Stroup recommended that the Conference provide in part the subsidy needed to bring this work to completion.

An Executive Committee was elected: Thomas B. Stroup to serve for 1948-1949; B. L. Ullman, 1948-1950; and Thomas H. English, 1948-1951. The Chairman and the Secretary would be *ex officiis* members of this Committee.

As dinner-guest of the Conference, Chancellor R. B. House of the University of North Carolina welcomed the Conference to Chapel Hill and stated his personal faith that literature, history, music, art, and religion keep human beings human, that is, show men how to live on the human level, rather than the level of either the medieval ascetic or the merely "economic man." To illustrate his point, he spoke of his pleasure in traditional folk music and played some of this music on his harmonica.

After the dinner, a motion was passed that a history of the Southern Humanities Conference be prepared to include brief histories of the constituent societies and statements of their aims and present activities. [The present bulletin contains this history.]

After discussion concerning the admission of new societies to membership in the Conference, the Chairman appointed a Committee on Standards of Admission: Kenneth W. Clark, Chairman, Albert G. A. Balz, and Arthur H. Moser.

The Southern Section of the Classical Association of the Middle West and South was asked to explore the feasibility of preparing a report on the teaching of the classics in the South. Mr. Sommer was requested to suggest to the Southeastern Conference of the College Art Association that it appoint a committee to interest colleges in sponsoring Southern exhibitions to foster the use of art in life. Mr. Sommer would bring back to the Conference suggestions as to how the Conference might help this committee.

Mr. English stated that, to be effective, the Southern Humanities Conference must be an evangelical body. He proposed that the Conference attempt to meet its many needs through employment of a full-time secretary to coordinate efforts already being made and to sponsor and make new efforts in support of the educational and cultural doctrines in which the group had faith. The Conference looked forward to doing evangelical work of this kind and, when possible, to establishing a central office with a full-time secretary.

A committee consisting of T. H. English, Chairman, E. E. Leisy, and L. R. Wilson was appointed to investigate ways and means of forming an advisory committee of men outside the teaching profession who would cooperate in carrying forward the work of the Conference.

## History

There was general discussion of three related problems: ways of attracting the best personnel to teach in the humanistic fields, of retaining the best teachers in the South in spite of the financial lures of institutions elsewhere, and of encouraging creative scholarship by means other than increased salaries. One difficulty in attracting brilliant young men to teach in the South is that instructorships in Southern institutions do not carry adequate salaries. Difficulties in keeping these young men, if they do come to the South, and in stimulating them to scholarly production lie in the scarcity of research grants, lack of travel-funds for attendance at scholarly meetings, and heavy teaching loads. The Conference resolved to urge that administrations include in their annual budgets ample funds and other provisions for research, fellowships, sabbatical leaves, and travel to professional meetings.

The Chairman reported that the American Council of Learned Societies had provided $2,000 a year for three years in partial support of the Southern Humanities Conference. With this figure in mind, the Conference set up a budget for the coming year, including provisions for publication of the Stroup Committee's Survey of Research in Progress, token support to the Committee on Americana, and support for the activities of the various committees.

\* \* \*

The Executive Committee of the Southern Humanities Conference met in Chapel Hill on October 22-23, 1948. Mr. Leavitt presented a letter from Mr. Parker, expressing regret that the Southern Association of Colleges and Secondary Schools could not become a member of the Conference, as it was contrary to the policy of the Association to send delegates to other organizations.

Mr. Stroup reported arrangements for publication of his

Survey of Research in Progress as Bulletin No. 1 of the Southern Humanities Conference. Mr. Leavitt reported progress of plans for Bulletin No. 2, a history of the Conference and its constituent societies. These bulletins would form the first of a series to be published by the University of North Carolina Press.

Ways of cooperating with the work of the American Council of Learned Societies in the South were discussed. It was suggested that members of the Conference seek ambitious young scholars, enlist their aid in carrying out the projects of the Conference, and help them with guidance and published recognition. It was decided to ask Earl Hartsell of the University of North Carolina, Secretary of the English Teachers' group of the N. C. Education Association, to prepare for the April meeting, a report on what was being done in stimulation of English teaching in the North Carolina high schools.

\* \* \*

The second meeting of the Southern Humanities Conference was held in Chapel Hill on April 22-23, 1949. Present were Sturgis E. Leavitt, Chairman; J. O. Bailey, Secretary; delegates Albert G. A. Balz, Kenneth W. Clark, T. D. Clark, Glen Haydon, E. E. Leisy, Arthur H. Moser, E. D. Myers (Philosophy, Roanoke College, replacing R. L. Patterson for the Southern Society for the Philosophy of Religion), Thomas B. Stroup, and Louis R. Wilson; members-at-large, W. C. Binkley, Thomas H. English, and B. L. Ullman. Present as visitors and observers were Robert M. Lester (the Carnegie Foundation for the Advancement of Teaching), John Marshall and Chadbourne Gilpatric (the Rockefeller Foundation), Charles E. Odegaard (Executive Director of the American Council of Learned Societies), Quentin O. McAllister (Romance Languages, Meredith College), and Earl Hartsell.

Mr. McAllister presented a report on an investigation of

the opinions of executives in business, industry, and governmental agencies, concerning the values of college work in foreign languages, English, and cultural subjects. The replies indicated that knowledge of a foreign language was important in business, that competence in writing English and an understanding of ideas expressed in literature had high value, and that cultural studies in the Humanities were conducive to executive competence. Some business firms expressed concern that many college graduates with competent training in the technical fields of business were handicapped by deficiencies in English. The Conference decided to encourage the publication of this report.

Mr. Hartsell presented the work of the North Carolina English Teachers' organization. It holds annual meetings in connection with the North Carolina Education Association, and separate meetings each fall; it has held seven annual Institutes as "summer revival meetings" to discuss methods, curricula, the place of research in English teaching, and similar topics. It publishes four issues each year of a magazine, *The North Carolina English Teacher*. The organization has supported standards of certification higher than those prevailing and had them accepted by the State Department of Public Instruction; it contributed most of the standards prescribed in the state's official bulletin, *Language Arts;* and its research committee has collected data concerned with folk-lore and proverbs, and effective means of teaching spelling. The organization has prepared a "Literary Map of North Carolina." It was decided that the Conference should do everything possible to encourage such groups as the North Carolina English Teachers, without assuming responsibility for promotion or direction of their work.

Mr. Bailey reported progress in the collection of data,

through circular letters of inquiry, for an index of societies in the South interested in the humanities. When the index was completed, he suggested that it might be useful to the Conference for securing information about research in progress, for publicity about the work of the Conference, and as a means for the discovery of non-college people engaged in research.

The Conference adjourned for dinner, as guests of the University of North Carolina. Chancellor House, presiding, welcomed the Conference and other guests. Mr. Odegaard, in an after-dinner talk, defined the fields of the Humanities and their values. After dinner, the members of the Conference repaired to the Communications Center where, as guests of the Radio and Music Departments of the University, they witnessed the performance of "Wherein Is Treasured and Renewed," a musical play broadcasting the importance of the Humanities today.

On Saturday morning, when the Conference reassembled, Mr. Lester described the Southern program of the Carnegie Foundation for the Advancement of Teaching. The program, he said, was based on the idea that a man who is doing research is a better teacher than one who is not. It was a cooperative plan with the Carnegie Corporation and the colleges and universities contributing. Four university centers had been set up in the South: at Nashville, New Orleans, Atlanta, and Durham-Chapel Hill considered as a unit. The university in each center associated with itself the colleges in its area; local committees selected the men to receive the awards. Grants were available to men who had completed their training, were active in teaching, and might use the grants to deepen, through research, their own background for teaching.

Mr. Wilson reported an investigation into the relationship of library resources to graduate work. Library resources have a definite, nearly measurable bearing upon the ability of institutions to support work for the doctorate, especially in relation to the number of fields in which the degree may be granted. The Southeast, he said, had about a dozen libraries adequate to support advanced research. Southern institutions were spending more on books and periodicals than ever before, but they were still behind because of the small bases from which they started.

Mr. Leavitt reported the results of his investigations into what Southern institutions were doing to encourage research. Replies to 250 letters outlined a wide variety of plans and methods for including research funds in their budgets and for allotting these funds. Mr. Leavitt proposed that the Conference proceed to a complete survey of what colleges in the South were doing for research and that the results of the survey be published, not as a statistical survey, but as a comparative study giving names and particulars about each institution. Mr. Odegaard supported Mr. Leavitt's suggestion as a point of strategy. He spoke of the Conference as an agency in the South, similar to the American Council in the nation, to combat indifference, inertia, and weaknesses of policy in regard to research and its adequate recognition and support. It was decided to continue the investigation and to publish the results.

Mr. English proposed the publication of a standard, basic reading list in English and American literature for high schools. Students in high schools today, he said, were not reading books; colleges could not assume, as in former years, that every student who came to college would be equipped with some knowledge of a few significant books. Various objections to the list were raised: differences in state standards, the fact that not all students who attend high school go to college, and probable disagreement on the length and contents of any recommended list. In spite of these objections the Conference approved the general idea that a list be worked out and given publicity.

Mr. Ullman reported on the survey of the teaching of classics in the South. The committee was examining requirements in Latin and Greek for various degrees, the numbers of majors in the classics, the numbers of graduate students, and the activities of teachers of Latin and Greek in research and in scholarly meetings.

Mr. Balz presented the nearly completed manuscript of his biographical and bibliographical study of teachers of philosophy in the South. The Chairman suggested that the study might include an interpretation of the teaching of philosophy and asked that the manuscript be sent to the Conference to be read by a committee.

Mr. Stroup exhibited Bulletin No. 1, now entitled *Humanistic Scholarship in the South*. George Stephens of Asheville, Editor of *The Southern Packet,* was the guest of the Conference during luncheon. He had brought with him, for distribution at the dinner the night before, copies of a review of Mr. Stroup's work written by Gerald W. Johnson and published in the *Packet*.

Kenneth W. Clark reported for the Committee on Standards of Admission that a constituent society should be regional, should represent one of the Humanities, should be concerned primarily with research and theory, should have a scholarly personnel, should have a stable and financially responsible organization, and should be active.

Mr. Stroup presented a report on the Check-List of Collections of Manuscripts and Rare Books in Southern Libraries, in preparation by Mr. Spivey's Committee on Americana. The Conference decided to assist in the publication of this checklist.

Mr. Bailey spoke of the fact that a large number of creative writers of national reputation live in the South, but that Southern libraries have made little effort to acquire and preserve their manuscripts. It was his opinion that many writers might be persuaded to give manuscripts to an interested library in the home-region. He suggested that a committee be appointed to pursue this matter and get manuscripts moving into Southern libraries. Mr. Stroup and Mr. Binkley approved the idea, but added the suggestion that historical documents as well as literary manuscripts should be included.

To replace Mr. Bailey, retiring as member-at-large, Fletcher M. Green was elected member-at-large. Mr. Leavitt was re-elected Chairman of the Conference, and Mr. Myers, Secretary. Mr. Stroup was re-elected to the Executive Committee. Kenneth W. Clark, retiring, announced that J. Philip Hyatt, Vanderbilt University, had been elected delegate to the Conference from the Southern Section of the Society of Biblical Literature and Exegesis.

\* \* \*

The Executive Committee met in Chapel Hill on November 5, 1949. Mr. English found it impossible to attend, but Messrs. Stroup, Ullman, Leavitt, and Myers plunged vigorously into the business before the Committee.

In reporting on the activities of the American Council of Learned Societies, Mr. Leavitt spoke of its study of university fellowships and grants-in-aid of research. He stated that the Conference could be useful to the American Council in surveying personnel in the Humanities in the South.

Mr. Myers reported that various colleges and universities in Virginia were planning a conference on the Humanities. He was instructed to offer the encouragement and support of the Southern Humanities Conference and to represent it at the proposed meeting.

Since the McAllister report on foreign languages and business was nearly complete, the Committee voted to ask Thomas B. Stroup, Francis C. Hayes (Spanish, University of Florida), and President H. Sherman Oberly of Roanoke College to read it and make recommendations concerning its publication.

It was thought that a list of non-academic "Friends of the Humanities" in the South might be useful to the Conference, the American Council of Learned Societies, and the Board of Control for Southern Regional Education. The Secretary was instructed to ask Marshall W. Fishwick of Washington and Lee to prepare such a list.

Louis R. Wilson spoke on the relation of library resources to graduate work in the South, prospects for improving these resources, and the lines that improvement should follow. Although the maintenance of adequate library facilities is a major problem in Southern higher education, he said that the Board of Control for Southern Regional Education was not immediately concerned with the improvement of library facilities. It was voted to notify John E. Ivey, Jr., Director of this Board, that the Southern Humanities Conference would offer the Board any help within its power.

After a discussion of ways and means of interesting Southern writers in depositing their manuscripts in libraries and of encouraging Southern libraries to collect and preserve such manuscripts, the Chairman was instructed to urge representative libraries to make active search for these materials.

It was voted to ask E. E. Leisy to prepare a preliminary report on finding and encouraging young Humanistic scholars in the South.

The invitation of President Colgate W. Darden, Jr., of the University of Virginia to hold the spring meeting on that campus was accepted.

\* \* \*

## History

The Southern Humanities Conference convened for its third annual meeting in the library of the Colonnade Club of the University of Virginia on April 14, 1950. Those present were: Sturgis E. Leavitt, Chairman; Edward D. Myers, Secretary; delegates Albert G. A. Balz, James Merton England (University of Kentucky), for the Southern Historical Association; Glen Haydon; S. Vernon McCasland (University of Virginia), for the Southern Section of the Society for Biblical Literature and Exegesis; Roger P. McCutcheon (Tulane University), for the South Central Modern Language Association; Arthur H. Moser; Clemens Sommer; Thomas B. Stroup; Miss Roy Land (University of Virginia), for the Southeastern Library Association; member-at-large Fletcher M. Green; and Donald H. Daugherty, observer for the American Council of Learned Societies.

Mr. Daugherty, introduced by the Chairman, spoke of the continued interest of the American Council in the work of the Conference, and in the general promotion of regional associations for the Humanities.

The Chairman announced that Mr. Fishwick of Washington and Lee had compiled a classified and annotated list of about 450 names of non-academic "Friends of the Humanities" in the South. The Chairman reported also that he had a list of Fellows of the American Council of Learned Societies and the Rockefeller Foundation, and a list of "Friends of the Humanities" engaged in teaching and scholarship in the South. It was voted that, besides other uses to be made of these lists, they be furnished to the placement officer of any college or university that becomes an Associate Member of the Southern Humanities Conference.

In the late afternoon, the Conference adjourned to the home of Professor and Mrs. Balz, where the members were delightfully entertained and introduced to a number of the faculty and administration of the University of Virginia. In the evening, members of the Conference were entertained at a dinner in the Rotunda, as guests of the University of Virginia. For these hospitalities and the cordial words of greeting from President Darden, the Conference adopted appropriate resolutions of appreciation and thanks.

In a resumed session, after the dinner, Mr. Myers reported that, as representative of the Conference, he had attended the meeting on the Humanities which had been held on March 17 at Hollins College, Virginia, with the encouragement and partly under the sponsorship of the Southern Humanities Conference. Twenty representatives from ten institutions had gathered, heard reports, discussed problems, and voted that a continuing conference be held in 1951. The Southern Humanities Conference recognized the Virginia Conference as an affiliate and voted to support it to a limited extent. The desirability of promoting similar state conferences was discussed, with general approval of the idea.

It was voted that the colleges and universities of the South be invited to become Institutional Associate Members of the Conference upon payment of an annual fee of $10.00. For this fee, the Conference would furnish each institutional member a copy of each Bulletin published, a copy of each report and of each completed research project, an occasional news-letter giving an account of work in progress, and copies of the minutes of the meetings of both the Conference and its Executive Committee.

Mr. Leavitt reported on the status of his investigation into Southern institutional support of research and provision for travelling expenses to professional meetings. He was authorized to continue this work, to seek from each institution an exact and particular statement, and to publish the results.

The Chairman reported that Mr. McAllister had completed the first draft of his investigation of the opinions of business, industry, and governmental agencies regarding the values of cultural studies. It was hoped that this report would appear in 1950 as Bulletin No. 3.

Miss Land reported on the current survey of the facilities of libraries in the South for graduate work. This survey is in preparation for the Board of Control for Southern Regional Education. The Chairman was requested to continue his work of encouraging libraries to secure and preserve the manuscripts of Southern writers, and to complete his survey of what libraries are doing about this matter.

Mr. Moser made a preliminary report on "The Status of the Classics in the South," describing the organization of committees to collect information in fourteen Southern states. Hope was expressed that the report would be completed and ready for publication in the fall of 1950.

Mr. Stroup reported on the compilation by C. H. Cantrell and W. R. Patrick of the Alabama Polytechnic Institute of "A Bibliography of Theses on Southern Literary Culture." This compilation is seeking to list all graduate theses written before August 30, 1948, at any graduate school in the United States on any aspect of Southern culture within the fields of English, history, languages, music, speech, and journalism. The bibliography is expected to be ready for publication by August 1, 1950.

The Chairman was authorized to seek $2,000 to promote two conferences on the improvement of the teaching of English in the South.

The Conference requested Mr. McCasland to prepare, for the 1951 meeting, a report on the Teaching of Religion and Biblical Literature in the South; Mr. Sommer to report on Art in the Humanities in the South; and Mr. Haydon, on Music in the Humanities in the South. The Conference requested the Executive Committee to secure some one to make a report on Humanities programs and courses in the colleges of the South.

The Conference accepted the invitation of Washington and Lee University to hold the 1951 meeting on its campus. Officers and a new member-at-large were elected: Chairman, Sturgis E. Leavitt; Secretary, Edward D. Myers; member-at-large, Douglas Southall Freeman of Richmond; and member of the Executive Committee, 1950-1953, Fletcher M. Green.

\* \* \*

One does not give the name "renaissance" to a period of revitalized scholarship and intellectual activity, until this scholarship and this activity have borne full fruit, and not even then, until it is perhaps on the decline and may be seen in retrospect. The foregoing record, briefly surveying the crowded agenda of the Southern Humanities Conference through its first few meetings, suggests more challenge than material for nostalgia. Much is being accomplished to vitalize the Humanities in the South; more remains to be done by the Conference and by other forces. The members of the Southern Humanities Conference feel that they have reason to be hopeful that their labors will bear fruit.

# MEETINGS AND OFFICERS
## PRELIMINARY MEETING
Chapel Hill, N. C.
*May 17-18, 1947*

J. O. Bailey (English), University of North Carolina, Adviser.

Kenneth W. Clark, representing the Southern Society of Biblical Literature and Exegesis.

T. D. Clark, President, Southern Historical Association.

Hardin Craig (English), University of North Carolina, Adviser.

Allan H. Gilbert, President, South Atlantic Modern Language Association.

B. v. H. Gilmer, President, Southern Society for Philosophy and Psychology.

Glen Haydon (Music), University of North Carolina, Adviser.

Jay B. Hubbell (English), Duke University, Adviser.

Louis O. Kattsoff (Philosophy), University of North Carolina, Adviser.

Sturgis E. Leavitt (Spanish), University of North Carolina, Adviser.

Loren C. MacKinney (History), University of North Carolina, Adviser.

Arthur H. Moser, President, Southern Section of the Classical Association of the Middle West and South.

James W. Patton, Secretary, Southern Historical Association.

George Pope Shannon, representing the Work Conference on Higher Education, Southern Association of Colleges and Secondary Schools.

Richard H. Shryock, Acting Director, American Council of Learned Societies.

Thomas B. Stroup, Chairman of Committee on the Humanities, South Atlantic Modern Language Association.

Charles S. Sydnor (History), Duke University, Adviser.

B. L. Ullman, representing the Southern Section of the Classical Association of the Middle West and South.

Joseph Weitz, Secretary, Southern Society for Philosophy and Psychology.

Louis R. Wilson, representing the Southeastern Library Association.

TEMPORARY OFFICERS ELECTED

Sturgis E. Leavitt, Chairman; J. O. Bailey, Secretary

\* \* \*

## ORGANIZATIONAL MEETING

*Duke University*
*October 25-26, 1947*

J. O. Bailey, Secretary *pro tem*.

Albert G. A. Balz, representing the Southern Society for Philosophy and Psychology.

Kenneth W. Clark, representing the Society of Biblical Literature and Exegesis.

T. D. Clark, representing the Southern Historical Association.

Hardin Craig (English), University of North Carolina, Adviser.

Allan H. Gilbert (English), Duke University, Adviser.

B. v. H. Gilmer, representing the Southern Society for Philosophy and Psychology.

Glen Haydon, representing the American Musicological Society.

Jay B. Hubbell (English), Duke University, Adviser.

ARTHUR P. HUDSON (English), University of North Carolina, Adviser.
LOUIS O. KATTSOFF (Philosophy), University of North Carolina, Adviser.
CORNELIUS KRUSÉ, Executive Director, American Council of Learned Societies.
STURGIS E. LEAVITT, Chairman *pro tem*.
LOREN C. MACKINNEY (History), University of North Carolina, Adviser.
ARTHUR H. MOSER, representing the Southern Section of the Classical Association of the Middle West and South.
ROSCOE E. PARKER, representing the Southern Association of Colleges and Secondary Schools.
JAMES W. PATTON, Secretary, Southern Historical Association.
THOMAS B. STROUP, representing the South Atlantic Modern Language Association.
B. L. ULLMAN (Classics), University of North Carolina, Adviser.
LOUIS R. WILSON, representing the Southeastern Library Association.

TEMPORARY OFFICERS ELECTED

STURGIS E. LEAVITT, Chairman; J. O. BAILEY, Secretary

\* \* \*

FIRST OFFICIAL MEETING
THE SOUTHERN HUMANITIES CONFERENCE

CHAPEL HILL, N. C.
*April 23-24, 1948*

J. O. BAILEY, University of North Carolina, Member-at-large.
ALBERT G. A. BALZ, Delegate, Southern Society for Philosophy and Psychology.

W. C. BINKLEY, Vanderbilt University, Member-at-large.

KENNETH W. CLARK, Delegate, Southern Section of the Society of Biblical Literature and Exegesis.

THOMAS H. ENGLISH, Emory University, Member-at-large.

FLETCHER M. GREEN (alternate for T. D. Clark, Delegate), Southern Historical Association.

GLEN HAYDON, Delegate, Southeastern Chapter of the American Musicological Association.

STURGIS E. LEAVITT, Delegate, American Council of Learned Societies.

ERNEST E. LEISY (alternate for ALLAN D. McKILLOP, Delegate), South-Central Modern Language Association.

ARTHUR H. MOSER, Delegate, Southern Section of the Classical Association of the Middle West and South.

ROSCOE E. PARKER, Observer for the Southern Association of Colleges and Secondary Schools.

R. L. PATTERSON, Delegate, Southern Society for the Philosophy of Religion.

CLEMENS SOMMER, Delegate, Southeastern Conference of the College Art Association.

THOMAS B. STROUP, Delegate, South Atlantic Modern Language Association.

B. L. ULLMAN, Delegate-at-large.

LOUIS R. WILSON, Delegate, Southeastern Library Association.

OFFICERS ELECTED

STURGIS E. LEAVITT, Chairman; J. O. BAILEY, Secretary

EXECUTIVE COMMITTEE

THOMAS H. ENGLISH (1948-1951); THOMAS B. STROUP (1948-1949); B. L. ULLMAN (1948-1950)

TERMS OF DELEGATES OF SOCIETIES

1948-1949—Kenneth W. Clark, Southern Section of the Society of Biblical Literature and Exegesis; E. E. Leisy, South-

Central Modern Language Association; Louis R. Wilson, Southeastern Library Association.

1948-1950—Glen Haydon, Southeastern Chapter of the American Musicological Association; Clemens Sommer, Southeastern Conference of the College Art Association; Thomas B. Stroup, South Atlantic Modern Language Association.

1948-1951—Albert G. A. Balz, Southern Society for Philosophy and Psychology; T. D. Clark, Southern Historical Association; Arthur H. Moser, Southern Section of the Classical Association of the Middle West and South; R. L. Patterson, Delegate, Southern Society for the Philosophy of Religion.

TERMS OF MEMBERS-AT-LARGE

1948-1949—J. O. BAILEY
1948-1950—B. L. ULLMAN
1948-1951—THOMAS H. ENGLISH AND
W. C. BINKLEY

\* \* \*

## SECOND ANNUAL MEETING
## SOUTHERN HUMANITIES CONFERENCE

CHAPEL HILL, N. C.
*April 22-23, 1949*

J. O. BAILEY, Secretary, Delegate-at-large.
ALBERT G. A. BALZ, Delegate, Southern Society for Philosophy and Psychology.
W. C. BINKLEY, Member-at-large.
KENNETH W. CLARK, Delegate, Southern Section of the Society of Biblical Literature and Exegesis.
T. D. CLARK, Delegate, Southern Historical Association.
THOMAS H. ENGLISH, Member-at-large.
CHADBOURNE GILPATRIC, Observer, The Rockefeller Foundation.

EARL HARTSELL, Observer, University of North Carolina.
GLEN HAYDON, Delegate, Southeastern Chapter of the American Musicological Association.
STURGIS E. LEAVITT, Chairman, representing the Americal Council of Learned Societies.
E. E. LEISY, Delegate, South Central Modern Language Association.
ROBERT M. LESTER, Observer, Carnegie Foundation for the Advancement of Teaching.
JOHN MARSHALL, Observer, The Rockefeller Foundation.
QUENTIN O. MCALLISTER, Observer, Meredith College, Raleigh, N. C.
ARTHUR H. MOSER, Delegate, Southern Section of the Classical Association of the Middle West and South.
E. D. MYERS, Delegate, Southern Society for the Philosophy of Religion.
CHARLES E. ODEGAARD, Executive Director, American Council of Learned Societies.
THOMAS B. STROUP, Delegate, South Atlantic Modern Language Association.
B. L. ULLMAN, Member-at-large.
LOUIS R. WILSON, Delegate, Southeastern Library Association.

OFFICERS ELECTED

STURGIS E. LEAVITT, Chairman; E. D. MYERS, Secretary

EXECUTIVE COMMITTEE

THOMAS H. ENGLISH (1948-1951); THOMAS B. STROUP (1949-1952); B. L. ULLMAN (1948-1950)

TERMS OF DELEGATES OF SOCIETIES

1948 1950—Glen Haydon, Southeastern Chapter of the American Musicological Association; Clemens Sommer, Southeastern Conference of the College Art Association; Thomas

*Meetings and Officers*  31

B. Stroup, South Atlantic Modern Language Association.

1948-1951—Albert G. A. Balz, Southern Society for Philosophy and Psychology; T. D. Clark, Southern Historical Association; E. D. Myers, Southern Society for the Philosophy of Religion; Arthur H. Moser, Southern Section of the Classical Association of the Middle West and South.

1949-1952—S. Vernon McCasland, Southern Section of the Society for Biblical Literature and Exegesis; Roger P. McCutcheon, South Central Modern Language Association; Louis R. Wilson, Southeastern Library Association.

TERMS OF MEMBERS-AT-LARGE
1948-1950—B. L. ULLMAN
1948-1951—THOMAS H. ENGLISH AND
W. C. BINKLEY
1949-1952—FLETCHER M. GREEN

\* \* \*

## THIRD ANNUAL MEETING
## SOUTHERN HUMANITITES CONFERENCE

CHARLOTTESVILLE, VA.
*April 14-15, 1950*

ALBERT G. A. BALZ, Delegate, Southern Society for Philosophy and Psychology.

D. H. DAUGHERTY, Observer for the American Council of Learned Societies.

JAMES MERTON ENGLAND (alternate for T. D. CLARK, Delegate), Southern Historical Association.

FLETCHER M. GREEN, Member-at-large.

GLEN HAYDON, Delegate, Southeastern Chapter of the American Musicological Association.

Miss Roy Land (Alternate for Louis R. Wilson, Delegate), Southeastern Library Association.

Sturgis E. Leavitt, Chairman, Delegate, American Council of Learned Societies.

S. Vernon McCasland, Delegate, Southern Section of the Society for Biblical Literature and Exegesis.

Roger P. McCutcheon, Delegate, South-Central Modern Language Association.

Arthur H. Moser, Delegate, Southern Section of the Classical Association of the Middle West and South.

E. D. Myers, Secretary, representing the Southern Society for the Philosophy of Religion.

Clemens Sommer, Delegate, Southern Classical Association.

Thomas B. Stroup, Delegate, South Atlantic Modern Language Association.

OFFICERS ELECTED

Sturgis E. Leavitt, Chairman; E. D. Myers, Secretary

EXECUTIVE COMMITTEE

Thomas H. English (1948-1951); Fletcher M. Green (1950-1953); Thomas B. Stroup (1949-1952)

TERMS OF DELEGATES OF SOCIETIES

1948-1951—Albert G. A. Balz, Southern Society for Philosophy and Psychology; T. D. Clark, Southern Historical Association; E. D. Myers, Southern Society for the Philosophy of Religion; Arthur H. Moser, Southern Section of the Classical Association of the Middle West and South.

1949-1952—S. Vernon McCasland, Southern Section of the Society for Biblical Literature and Exegesis; Roger P. McCutcheon, South-Central Modern Language Association; Louis R. Wilson, Southeastern Library Association.

1950-1953—Delegate of the Southeastern Chapter of the

American Musicological Association; Delegate of the Southeastern Conference of the College Art Association; Delegate of the South Atlantic Modern Language Association.

TERMS OF MEMBERS-AT-LARGE

1948-1951—THOMAS H. ENGLISH AND
W. C. BINKLEY

1949-1952—FLETCHER M. GREEN

1950-1953—DOUGLAS SOUTHALL FREEMAN

# HISTORIES OF THE CONSTITUENT SOCIETIES

# HISTORIES OF THE CONSTITUENT SOCIETIES

## THE AMERICAN MUSICOLOGICAL SOCIETY
### SOUTHEASTERN CHAPTER

On June 3, 1934, nine people—George Dickinson, Carl Engel, Gustave Reese, Helen Roberts, Joseph Schillinger, Charles Seeger, Harold Spivacke, Oliver Strunk, and Joseph Yasser—met in New York and formed the American Musicological Society. Otto Kinkeldey was elected President. The first general meeting was held in the Beethoven Association Club Rooms on December 1 of that year, and a constitution and by-laws were drawn up. There are now ten regional chapters—New England, Greater New York, Western New York, Philadelphia, Southeastern, Midwestern, Northwestern, Northern California, Southern California, and Texas.

There are about 650 members in the national association. The states included in the Southeastern Chapter are Maryland, North Carolina, and Virginia. This chapter has about 50 members. The American Musicological Society is an association of musical scholars and persons interested in the systematic study of music as an art, as a science, and as a branch of learning. The Society carries out its activities through meetings at which papers are read by members, through the sponsoring of special musical performances, through publications, and through the work of its members in many fields of musical research.

The Society is international in scope. It has members in several countries of Europe, in Canada, and in Latin America. In 1939 the Society sponsored an International Congress in New York, which was attended by eminent musicologists of various nationalities. The Society keeps in close touch with musicological activities throughout the world and welcomes an exchange of information and data with similar organizations in other countries. The present (1950) officers of the Society are President, David Stone, 4945 Brandywine Street, N.W., Washington, D. C., and Secretary, Minnie Elmer, 1830 Lamont Street, N.W., Washington, D. C.

The national organization publishes the *Journal of the American Musicological Society,* founded in 1948, which appears in April, August, and November. Its editor is Donald Grout, Department of Music, Cornell University, Ithaca, N. Y. The magazine has a circulation of about 900. It carries scholarly articles and extensive reviews by musicologists; and has an international coverage of news of musicological activity.

## THE CLASSICAL ASSOCIATION OF THE MIDDLE WEST AND SOUTH

### SOUTHERN SECTION

The Classical Association of the Middle West and South was founded through the activities of W. G. Manly of the University of Missouri. His original proposal met with great enthusiasm and the first meeting for organization was held in Chicago, May 5-6, 1905. The Association includes in its territory thirty states as well as the Canadian province of Ontario. Membership is open to teachers and students of the classical languages and allied fields and to others who have an interest in the support of the classics. Total membership at the present time is approximately 2,600.

The Association was created to provide for a union of kindred spirits, to further research in the classical areas and to furnish a forum for the discussion of such findings, to improve methods of teaching on both the collegiate and secondary levels, to offer through its official publication an additional channel for presenting material of interest to the membership, and to provide useful suggestions and encouragement especially to the widely separated teachers of Latin in the high schools.

In addition to continuous activity in matters pertaining to classical studies in general, the Association encouraged the Classical Investigation, which issued its momentous report in 1924, and has publicized and favored adherence to the findings and recommendations of the Investigation. Between 1934 and 1944 the Association, through its Committee on the Present Status of Classical Studies, conducted a campaign of investigation and publicity to unify the classical forces in its territory and within other classical associations for the purpose of improving instruction and of promoting the study of Latin in the schools as an integral part of general education. An annual "Latin Week" was promoted which has since become a national institution. In 1945 a Committee on Educational Policies was created which has been the prime mover in a project to realign Latin instruction, and to explore the possibility of introducing the reading of Vergil as the first major author in secondary Latin. There are also committees active in the creation and handling of scholarships and grants (Delcamp and Semple Awards) to provide able students and teachers with the opportunity for further study in graduate school, at the American Academy in Rome, and at the American School in Athens.

The Association's publication is *The Classical Journal*. It was founded, together with the Association, by the same group of interested Classicists, and the first number appeared in December, 1905. Membership in the Association ($3.75 a year) includes subscription to the *Journal*. This publication appears monthly in eight numbers from October through

May; the circulation is approximately 3,500. The *Journal* publishes few learned articles; it offers articles of more general interest, book reviews, notes, miscellanies, announcements, and such materials as will make it chiefly an organ for the use of teachers and their classes in the high schools. In this respect, it is unique among classical publications. The present editor is Clyde Murley, Northwestern University, Evanston, Illinois.

The Southern Section of the Classical Association of the Middle West and South had its inception when, at the regular meeting of the parent Classical Association in Atlanta in 1919, a plan was presented for the creation of a Southern branch of the society for the purpose of fostering and promoting interest in classical studies in that section of the country. When the Association met in Cleveland in the spring of 1920, the formation of a Southern branch was authorized, an appropriation was granted to help defray expenses, and a committee was empowered to proceed with the organization and arrange for the first meeting.

The committee was composed of the following representatives: Josiah B. Game, Florida State College for Women, Chairman; George Howe, University of North Carolina; W. D. Hooper, University of Georgia; R. B. Steele, Vanderbilt University; Herbert C. Lipscomb, Randolph-Macon Woman's College; E. L. Green, University of South Carolina; W. B. Saffold, University of Alabama; David M. Key, Millsaps College; and E. A. Bechtel, Tulane University. The first annual meeting of the Southern Section was held at Columbia, S. C., February 24-26, 1921, under the chairmanship of Josiah B. Game.

The Southern Section of the Classical Association of the Middle West and South is at all times a part of the parent organization and represents particularly the membership of the Association resident in the Southern states. The organization draws its members from fourteen Southern states: Alabama, Arkansas, Florida, Georgia, Kentucky, Louisiana, Mississippi, North Carolina, Oklahoma, South Carolina, Tennessee, Texas, Virginia, West Virginia. There are about one hundred members active in the meetings, although there are approximately five hundred members from the South in the Classical Association of the Middle West and South.

The Classical Association of the Middle West and South meets each year at a time which is close to the academic Easter vacation. The Southern Section meets, in years when the parent organization holds its meeting beyond the limits of the South, during the Thanksgiving vacation in various localities, always in the South.

Officers of the Classical Association of the Middle West and South are: President, Clarence A. Forbes, Ohio State University, Columbus, Ohio; First Vice-President, Miss Esther Weightman, Madison, Wisconsin; Secretary-Treasurer, William C. Korfmacher, St. Louis University, St. Louis, Mo. Current officers of the Southern Section are: President, Russel Geer, Tulane University, New Orleans, La.; Vice-President, Donnis Martin, Winthrop College, Rock Hill, S. C.; and Secretary-Treasurer, Graydon Regenos, Tulane University, New Orleans, La.

## THE COLLEGE ART ASSOCIATION

### SOUTHEASTERN REGIONAL CONFERENCE

The Southeastern College Art Conference was founded in March, 1941, at the request of the College Art Association of America, so as to have a Regional Art Conference in the Southeast, comparable to those of the Middle West and the Ohio Valley. The purpose was to afford meetings for conference and consultation on the broad fields of art teaching in the colleges and universities, and history of art and studio work, and for discussion of more local problems in the field. The further purpose of greater ease in assembling in more restricted geographical areas was in mind, for it was, and is, difficult for art teachers from all over the United States to assemble in any given city for the annual meeting of the College Art Association.

The states included in the Southeastern College Art Conference are Alabama, Florida, Georgia, Kentucky, Louisiana, North Carolina, South Carolina, Tennessee, and Virginia. The annual meeting is held during the last two weeks of March.

The aims of the Society are (1) to interpret a living and growing art interest in colleges and universities as they grow and change; (2) to serve as a sounding board for opinions on art and the teaching of art in colleges and universities; (3) to stimulate ways of improving and pointing directions for art on college and university campuses; (4) to develop common understanding of basic problems and bring about relationships which will strengthen the art programs in meeting the needs of students; and (5) to coordinate the work of this organization with other organizations interested in art so as to facilitate ways and means of working together.

The following officers are serving at the present time: President, Edmund Yaghjian, University of South Carolina; Vice-President, Ralph Wickiser, University of Louisiana; Secretary-Treasurer, Dawn S. Kennedy, Alabama College.

The 1950 meeting was held in Greensboro, North Carolina, and was attended by members from thirty-two colleges and universities from the nine southeastern states.

## THE SOCIETY OF BIBLICAL LITERATURE AND EXEGESIS

### SOUTHERN SECTION

The Society of Biblical Literature and Exegesis is a national organization, with a number of its members scattered throughout the world. It was founded in New York City in 1880, by a group of eight scholars—C. A. Briggs, F. Gardner, D. R. Goodwin, I. I. Mombert, Philip Schaff, Charles Short, James Strong, and E. A. Washburn—who enlisted thirty-three members the first year. There are now about one thousand members, including about ninety foreign members.

The object of the Society is "to stimulate the critical study of the Scriptures by presenting, discussing, and publishing original papers on Biblical subjects." This object has come to be interpreted broadly, including research into all phases of civilization in the Middle East, both pre-Biblical and Biblical. The main areas of study are language and literature, history of life and thought, social studies, and archaeology and textual criticism.

A permanent agency of the national society is the American Textual Criticism Seminar (est. 1946), of which Kenneth W. Clark was the executive secretary for 1948-1949. A Committee on Aid to German Scholars has been active since 1946, under Emil G. Kraeling.

The Society publishes quarterly (March, June, September, and December) the *Journal of Biblical Literature* (subscription, $6.00 per year; circulation, 1,400), now in its 67th volume, and also a monograph series, under the editorship of Robert C. Dentan, 4 Mansfield St., New Haven, Conn. The March issue of the *Journal* includes the Proceedings with abstracts of papers read at the national meeting, and also the Proceedings of the four sections. Many of the articles throughout the year are papers presented at an annual meeting of the Society or one of its sections, although some articles are submitted *de novo*. Most of the authors are members of the Society, although there is no restrictive policy.

The Society has established four sections: Midwest (1936), Canadian (1939), Pacific Coast (1941), and Southern (1948). The Southern Section has about two hundred members, from as far west as Texas and cutting across through Oklahoma, Arkansas, Kentucky, and Virginia.

At the present time there are over 240 members in the Southern Section of the Society of Biblical Literature and Exegesis. Its officers for 1950 are: President, David E. Faust, Catawba College, Salisbury, N. C.; Vice-President, Samuel Sandmel, Vanderbilt University, Nashville, Tennessee; and Secretary, Charles Nesbitt, Wofford College, Spartanburg, S. C.

## THE SOUTH ATLANTIC MODERN LANGUAGE ASSOCIATION

On Saturday, December 29, 1928, there assembled at the Henry Grady Hotel in Atlanta, Georgia, representatives of the modern language teachers from North and South Carolina, Georgia and Florida. W. S. Barney of the Woman's College of the University of North Carolina, Chairman of the Committee on Organization, had issued the call for the establishment of an association of modern language teachers. At this meeting the South Atlantic Modern Language Association came into being. Its first president was W. S. Barney, and its first secretary was T. Scott Holland. Vice-presidents for the various states represented were appointed: R. C. Deal for North Carolina, Adolphe Vermont for South Carolina, C. F. Hamff for Georgia, and E. V. Gage for Florida. The practice of multiple vice-presidents was discontinued as the Association gained strength, and it now has only one.

Alabama, Tennessee, and Kentucky came into the Association later, Kentucky being the last state admitted, in 1949. At the organizational meeting the date for the annual meeting was set for the Friday and Saturday immediately following Thanksgiving, and this practice has been adhered to ever since. Dues were set at one dollar a year, another practice which has not changed. When the official organ of the Association, the *South Atlantic Bulletin,* was founded, the annual dues included a subscription to this publication.

In 1932 the Association had grown to include 166 members. Today there are 864 members in good standing, and 85 libraries receiving the *Bulletin.*

The Association was founded for the purpose of advancing scholarship, teaching, and research in the modern languages and literatures in the states of the South Atlantic area. It is an organization of the teachers of English, of the modern foreign languages, of folklore, of comparative literature, and of allied fields. The Association aims at closer ties among the language teachers of the area it represents, and affords its members an opportunity at the annual meetings to exchange ideas and to keep in touch with the scholarly work being carried on at sister institutions.

The annual meeting of the Association is devoted primarily to section meetings for the various languages and for folklore and comparative literature. At these section meetings papers are presented by the members. Discussion circles in various fields are also held. These encompass a smaller group than the section meetings and are designed to stimulate discussion and research. At the annual meeting there also take place a general business session and a meeting of the Executive Committee of the Association. The latter consists of the president, the vice-president, the secretary-treasurer, the retiring president, and three members of the Association elected at large and serving for two years each. It is one of the duties of the Executive Committee to decide the place of the annual meeting. Member institutions issue invitations to the Association to meet on their campuses and act as gracious hosts at an annual luncheon. Thus members of the Association come to know their sister institutions, a chance very few of them might otherwise have.

The Association does not limit its activities to the presentation of papers at the annual meeting. It has a standing committee on the Humanities and on Americana. It is a participant in the Southern Humanities Conference, and has an active UNESCO Committee to keep its members in touch with the international organization and the benefits to be derived from it.

The official organ of the Association, the *South Atlantic Bulletin,* was published for the first time in May, 1935. It is through this publication that the Association provides the most for its members. Published quarterly, with various supplements as the occasion demands, the *Bulletin* keeps members informed of happenings in the area, and changes of staff at the various institutions, and affords the members data pertinent to their interests. It features descriptions of interesting collections in the libraries of the region served by the Association. It publishes an annual list of theses written by students at the associational institutions. A bibliography of Southern literary culture is an important contribution of the *Bulletin*. The *Bulletin* also finds occasion to publish a periodic list of publications by members of the Association. Through these services, as well as through its annually published membership list, the *Bulletin* serves as the cementing force for the members of the South Atlantic Modern Language Association.

The present officers (1950) of the South Atlantic Modern Language Association are: President, George B. Watts, Davidson College; Secretary-Treasurer, Sam Shiver, Emory University; Editor of the *South Atlantic Bulletin,* Sturgis E. Leavitt, University of North Carolina.

## THE SOUTH-CENTRAL MODERN LANGUAGE ASSOCIATION

The South-Central Modern Language Association was formed in New Orleans on December 28, 1939, at the time that the Modern Language Association of America met there. It came into being as a result of the remoteness of the region from centers in which the annual meetings of the national association were held, a remoteness which worked particular hardship on those of lower academic ranks, who, though eager to make contributions to the programs were unable to take expensive trips and thus lost encouragement to carry on their research. At the initial meeting Sturgis E. Leavitt was present and gave the group the benefit of his experience with the South Atlantic Modern Language Association. Roger P. McCutcheon of Tulane University was chosen Chairman, and A. P. Elliot of Southwestern Louisiana Institute, Secretary. These men were entrusted with setting up the organization.

The first regular meeting was held in Shreveport, Louisiana, November 1-2, 1940, on the invitation of Centenary College. Six states were represented: Louisiana, Texas, Oklahoma, Arkansas, Mississippi, and Tennessee. This is still the same territory in which the South-Central Modern Language Association operates. The registration at this meeting reached 212. Carleton Brown, former Secretary of the Modern Language Association, brought the blessing of the national association, and Gilbert Chinard and R. H. Griffith added philosophical breadth by their papers. The present membership of the association is 797. The annual meeting is held early in November.

Because of the war, no meetings were held from 1942 until 1946. The *South-Central Bulletin,* founded in December, 1940, continued to appear, however, and kept the organization together. Its first editor was Roger P. McCutcheon of Tulane University and the present editor is R. M. Lumiansky of Tulane University. The *Bulletin* appears in January, May, and October. Membership in the South-Central Modern Language Association costs $1.00 a year and includes subscription to the *Bulletin.* This publication is sent to libraries at the same rate. It contains reports of the annual meeting, notices of other meetings, book reviews, an anuual statement of Southern library holdings, lists of theses accepted in the South-Central states, and news of scholarly activities of its members.

The officers for 1949-1950 are: President, Leonard Beach, Oklahoma University; Vice-President, G. Waldo Dunnington, Northwestern Louisiana College; and Secretary-Treasurer, Jewel Wurtzbaugh, Oklahoma University.

## THE SOUTHEASTERN LIBRARY ASSOCIATION

The Southeastern Library Association was established at Signal Mountain, Tennessee, in the autumn of 1920 and adopted a formal constitution in 1922 at its second biennial meeting. It grew out of a proposal made by a group of Southern librarians in the summer of 1920 who were on their way to a meeting of the American Library Association at Colorado Springs. The group was interested in the formation of a library conference "small enough for close contacts and free discussion, and giving opportunity to consider library problems in the light of Southern conditions, social and economic, and taking into account the stage of library development in the South."

From the outset the conference has concerned itself with general problems and with policy making. In 1922, it decided to limit its activities to the consideration of ways and means of promoting library development. At its meeting in 1926, with representatives present from the General Education Board, the Southern Association of Colleges and Secondary Schools, and the American Library Association, it proposed and set in motion a chain of events designed to achieve genuine library development throughout the entire region. Three years later it appointed a policy committee to see that the program was properly formulated and carried out.

Some of the most important steps taken were as follows: In 1926, the over-all library development of the Southeast was carefully surveyed. Libraries in the region were found to be less extensively developed than anywhere else in the nation. The Southern Association of Colleges and Secondary Schools was asked to formulate, adopt, and enforce standards for high school libraries so that the oncoming generation of students would benefit from the use of library materials. A committee was appointed to carry out this program. It organized in 1926, and the Southern Association adopted school library standards in 1927.

Between 1927 and 1930, the General Education Board underwrote the establishment of the position of school library supervisor in a half dozen state departments of education or state library commissions in the Southeast. This insured skilled supervision of school libraries for a period of five years, after which it was expected that the support of the offices would be taken over by the states.

In 1929, the Julius Rosenwald Fund was invited to set aside $500,000 for the conduct of demonstration libraries throughout the South which would serve all the population, white and black, urban and rural, adult and juvenile, in school and out. Eleven counties were selected and the program was underwritten for a period of five years, each county undertaking to maintain library service on the basis of public support at fifty cents per capita. The Carnegie Corporation of New York financed a survey of appropriate agencies to train school librarians and provided funds for the support of a library field agent who maintained contacts with all types of libraries in the region from 1930 to 1935.

Permanent library schools were established through the assistance of educational foundations at William and Mary College, the University of North Carolina, George Peabody College for Teachers, and Louisiana State University, and curriculums in library subjects were also developed in many other institutions. As the training program got under way, state departments of education formulated and adopted library regulations for all the public schools of the region.

Since 1935, the Association has aided in forming other patterns of development. The Tennessee Valley Authority developed a new type of library cooperation in the seven states served by it. The Works Progress Administration, with its hundreds of paid workers and its many bookmobiles and deposit stations, brought library service to thousands in the South who had never used libraries before, and answered for all time the question whether Southerners would read if given the opportunity. State aid for school libraries was provided by a number of states, and state aid for public and county libraries has been secured generally throughout the region. State library extension agencies have been strengthened; modern library legislation has been generally enacted within the region; college and university libraries have greatly increased their resources for instruction and research; library associations for Negroes have been organized in three states; and library schools for the training of school, college, and public librarians for Negroes have been established at Hampton Institute, now discontinued, the North Carolina College at Durham, and Atlanta University.

The Association embraces the following states: Alabama, Florida, Georgia, Kentucky, Mississippi, North Carolina, South Carolina, Tennessee, and Virginia. It has no membership dues. For the transaction of business at the biennial meeting any person may vote who is a member of a State Association belonging to the Southeastern Library Association. There are about 2,500 members in the Association. Its present (1950) officers are: President, Clarence R. Graham, Free Public Library, Louisville, Ky.; Vice-President, Miss Elinor G. Preston, Director of School Libraries, Richmond, Va.; and Secretary-Treasurer, W. P. Kellam, Library of the University of Georgia, Athens, Ga.

The Association does not publish a magazine. Since 1926 it has published the *Papers and Proceedings* of its biennial meetings held usually in the autumn of even years. These contain the program, the principal papers or summaries, and the minutes of the meetings of the Association and of its various divisions. They are made available to each member. Unless they are out of print, back numbers can be secured from the Secretary.

## THE SOUTHERN HISTORICAL ASSOCIATION

Several years of casual discussion of the desirability of organizing members of the historical profession in the South, and persons elsewhere interested in Southern regional history, culminated in a meeting of representative historians in Atlanta, Georgia, on November 2, 1934. Charles M. Knapp of the University of Kentucky, Philip M. Hamer of the University of Tennessee, Thomas P. Abernethy of the University of Virginia, and Benjamin B. Kendrick of the Woman's College of the University of North Carolina took the initiative in calling the meeting. Favorable responses were received, and on the appointed date, the following persons assembled: Kathryn T. Abby, Florida State College for Women; Kathleen Bruce, Hollins College; John B. Clark, Mercer University; E. Merton Coulter, University of Georgia; Philip Davidson, Agnes Scott College; Edwin A. Davis, Louisiana State University; Dorothy Dodd, Tallahassee, Florida; Jonathan T. Dorris, State Teachers College, Richmond, Kentucky; Fletcher M. Green, Emory University; Philip M. Hamer, University of Tennessee; Theodore H. Jack, Randolph-Macon College; Charles M. Knapp, University of Kentucky; Ross H. McLean, Emory University; C. Lisle Percy, Piedmont College; George Petrie, Alabama Polytechnic Institute; Walter B. Posey, Birmingham-Southern College; Auxford S. Sartain, State Teachers College, Troy, Alabama; and Wendell H. Stephenson, Louisiana State University. The group organized the Southern Historical Association, adopted a constitution and by-laws, elected officers for 1935, and provided for the publication of a quarterly journal of history.

The major objectives of the Association are the promotion of interest and research in history, with particular emphasis on the history of the South; the collection and preservation of the South's historical records; and the encouragement and stimulation of state and local historical societies to more vigorous activity. A secondary purpose of the Association is to foster, through annual meetings, the study and teaching of all branches of history. The policies of the Association are formulated and its activities directed by an elective Executive Council. The officers elected for 1935 were: President, E. Merton Coulter; Vice-President, Thomas P. Abernethy; and Secretary-Treasurer, Charles M. Knapp.

The Association was enabled to publish a quarterly review of history through a guaranty provided by the Louisiana State University. After some years Vanderbilt University relieved Louisiana State of its obligation. In 1948 the University of Kentucky assumed the responsibility and currently aids in financing the *Journal of Southern History,* official organ of the Association. The managing editor, editorial associate, and board of editors are elected by the Executive Council. The Council controls the policy of the *Journal.* Wendell H. Stephenson was chosen the first editor, with Edwin A. Davis as associate editor. The original board of editors was composed of Thomas P. Abernethy, William C. Binkley, E. Merton Coulter, Dwight L. Dumond, Fletcher M. Green, Philip M. Hamer, Richard H. Shryock, and Charles S. Sydnor. Fred C. Cole later replaced Davis as editorial associate, and still later served as editor. When Vanderbilt University became the guarantor of the *Journal,* William C. Binkley became editor and Henry L. Swint, editorial associate. Since the University of Kentucky has been the guarantor, Thomas D. Clark has been editor and J. Merton England, associate editor. The first issue of the *Journal of Southern History* appeared in February, 1935; it has been published regularly in February, May, August, and November since that date, and is now in its sixteenth year.

Under the able editorship of Wendel H. Stephenson, the *Journal of Southern History* quickly attained an enviable position among scholarly periodicals, and it has continued to maintain its early high standards. The *Journal* contains articles based on original research in the history of the South, book reviews, bibliographical information, original documents, and personal news of interest to the historical profession.

The annual meetings of the Association, generally held in late October or early November, are devoted to papers and discussion of topics or problems in Southern regional history and general United States, Latin American, English, and European history. At the first annual meeting held in Birmingham, Alabama, in October, 1935, the Secretary reported a total of 354 members. Since that date the Association has had a rapid and continuous expansion. The present membership is 1,575. Active members are found in every state of the Union, except three, and in several foreign countries. Membership dues are $4.00 annually, and include a subscription to the *Journal of Southern History*. The Association has seventy-three exchange members, and the *Journal* circulates in every state of the American union and in Australia, Canada, China, England, France, Puerto Rico, and Scotland.

In 1945 the Executive Council of the Southern Historical Association authorized a special committee on research and in 1946 appropriated $500 for a survey of research needs in Southern history. The Committee, composed of William C. Binkley, Lester J. Cappon, Thomas D. Clark, E. Merton Coulter, Fletcher M. Green, Alfred J. Hanna, Ella Lonn, James W. Patton, Wendell H. Stephenson, and Charles S. Sydnor, held meetings in 1945, 1946, 1947, and 1948, and finally drew up a report on "Research Possibilities in Southern History," which is soon to be published in the *Journal of Southern History*. The report puts special emphasis on the need for study and research in various aspects of social and cultural history, including the church and religion, journalism, publication activities, cultural associations, and the fine arts. It is to be hoped that this report will bear fruit in the publication of many studies bearing on the humanities in the South.

The officers of the Southern Historical Association for 1950 are: President, William C. Binkley, Vanderbilt University; Vice-President, Avery O. Craven, University of Chicago; Secretary-Treasurer, J. Carlyle Sitterson, University of North Carolina; Editor, the *Journal of Southern History,* Thomas D. Clark, University of Kentucky.

## THE SOUTHERN SOCIETY FOR THE PHILOSOPHY OF RELIGION

The Southern Society for the Philosophy of Religion was organized in 1937 at Blue Ridge Assembly by a group of men interested in developing a philosophical interest in religion in the South. Among those who helped to inaugurate the organization were Edgar S. Brightman of Boston University, Henry N. Wieman of the University of Chicago, W. P. Warren of Bucknell University, and George B. Myers of the University of the South. Messrs. Brightman and Wieman, as representatives of universities outside the South, kept their interest in the Society but never constituted a part of its membership.

The Society continued to meet at Blue Ridge until war conditions made that impossible, and then it had a series of meetings at university centers. In 1943, the meeting was held at Chapel Hill; in 1944, at Chattanooga; and in 1945, at Emory University. The last three meetings have been held at Blue Ridge. The annual meeting is held during the third week of June.

The Society at present has sixty-two members and annual elections are made to the organization from professors of philosophy, professors of theology, and clergymen who are technical experts in the field of the philosophy of religion. It is presupposed that members have had considerable graduate work in the fields of either philosophy or theology. Members are drawn from the states south of the Mason and Dixon Line and east of the Mississippi River.

The purpose of the organization is both philosophical and religious. It is a society which exists to stimulate a technical philosophical study of religion, but it also desires to enrich religious life and experience through the instrumentality of an adequate philosophical study. The Society does not espouse social or political causes, or theological parties, but it is an open forum for the discussion of the great issues of the philosophy of religion.

The present (1950) officers are: President, J. R. Cresswell, University of West Virginia, Morgantown; Vice-President, Godfrey Tietze, University of Chattanooga, Chattanooga, Tennessee; and Secretary-Treasurer, James A. Rikard, Roanoke College, Salem, Va.

## THE SOUTHERN SOCIETY FOR PHILOSOPHY AND PSYCHOLOGY

The founding of this Society may appropriately be dated February 8, 1904, when Edward Franklin Buchner sought by letter the advice of such men as William James, J. McKeen Cattell, George Trumbull Ladd, and J. Mark Baldwin with respect to the establishment of an organization to comprise the psychologists and philosophers of the Southern region. It is recorded that a preliminary conference was held at the meeting of the Department of Superintendence of the National Educational Association at Atlanta on February 23, 1904, and that the first officers were selected then.

The polymorphus titles of the nine men at the first conference indicate their academic environment at the time. Besides Mr. Buchner, then Professor of Philosophy and Education at the University of Alabama, there were James Mark Baldwin, Professor of Philosophy and Psychology from the recently re-established laboratory at Johns Hopkins; B. B. Breese, Professor of Psychology and Ethics at the University of Tennessee; H. E. Brierly, Professor of Experimental Psychology and Biology at Florida State College; A. C. Ellis, Adjunct Professor of the Science and Art of Education at the University of Texas; A. R. Hill, Dean of the Teachers' College at the University of Mississippi; R. P. Halleck, Principal of the Boys' High School at Louisville, Ky.; W. Rose, Professor of Philosophy and Education at the University of Tennessee; and William T. Harris, United States Commissioner of Education. For five years Professor Buchner was the Secretary-Treasurer of the Society, and became its President in 1910. The first annual meeting was held at the Johns Hopkins University on December 27, 1904. Since 1915 the meetings have been held in the spring, immediately before Easter.

The broad objectives of the Society are represented, in the phrase of an earlier constitution, as that of promoting the interests of "psychology, philosophy, and experimental education in the southern section of the United States." In the language of the present constitution its aims are: ". . . to promote Philosophy and Psychology in the Southern section of the United States by facilitating the exchange of ideas among those engaged in these fields of inquiry, by encouraging investigation, by fostering the educational function of Philosophy and Psychology, and by improving the academic status of these subjects."

In the days of the founding of the Society philosophical and psychological teaching and inquiry were not so far apart as they have since become. Many, probably most, of the earlier members were teachers and investigators in both fields. In many instances, philosophy and psychology were combined within a single institutional department, and often the name of the department involved only the word "philosophy."

Despite the so-called emancipation of Psychology elsewhere, the tradition of the Society persisted. The relative independence of Psychology with respect to Philosophy, and, for that matter, of Philosophy with respect to Psychology, continues in the work of this Society to be viewed as a functional distinction, largely determined by practical considerations, rather than as a separation inherent in the nature of the two enterprises of mind. In recent years the membership has changed to such an extent that the "philosophers" form a minority. Some twenty years ago concurrent sections for Philosophy and for Psychology became the practice at the annual meetings, whereas previously both fields were represented in every division of the program. As a survival of this traditional practice the annual meeting now closes with a joint session in which various aspects of the relationship of the two fields are usually subject to discussion. As a symbol of its conviction that cooperation between the philosopher and the psychologist is theoretically necessary and practically stimulating, and that the conjunction of these fields persists except in theoretical abstraction, the Society maintains its tradition of alternating the office of president, while its Council always comprises both philosophers and psychologists.

The present officers of the Southern Society for Philosophy and Psychology are: President, Lewis M. Hammond, University of Virginia; Secretary, Maurice D. Allan, Hampden-Sydney College; Treasurer, Richard H. Henneman, University of Virginia. The number of members is approximately four hundred.

# THE SOUTHERN HUMANITIES CONFERENCE

# ASSOCIATE MEMBERS

In accordance with a vote passed at the meeting of the Southern Humanities Conference held in Charlottesville, Va., in April, 1950, the colleges and universities in the South were invited to become associate members of the Conference. The following institutions, with the names of their faculty representatives, have accepted:

FURMAN UNIVERSITY, Greenville, S. C.
  Dr. R. N. Daniel
LONGWOOD COLLEGE, Farmville, Va.
  President Dabney S. Lancaster
LOUISIANA STATE UNIVERSITY, Baton Rouge, La.
  Dean C. G. Taylor
LYNCHBURG COLLEGE, Lynchburg, Va.
  President Orville M. Wake
MARY BALDWIN COLLEGE, Staunton, Va.
  Dean Martha Grafton
RADFORD COLLEGE, Radford, Va.
  Dr. William S. Long
RANDOLPH-MACON WOMAN'S COLLEGE, Lynchburg, Va.
  President Theodore S. Jack
ROANOKE COLLEGE, Salem, Va.
  President H. Sherman Oberly
SOUTHWESTERN LOUISIANA INSTITUTE, Lafayette, La.
  President Joel L. Fletcher
UNIVERSITY OF FLORIDA, Gainesville, Fla.
  Dean Ralph E. Page
UNIVERSITY OF KENTUCKY, Lexington, Ky.
  Professor M. M. White

UNIVERSITY OF MISSISSIPPI, University, Miss.
    Dean Pete Kyle Carter
UNIVERSITY OF NORTH CAROLINA, Chapel Hill, N. C.
    Chancellor Robert B. House
UNIVERSITY OF THE SOUTH, Sewanee, Tenn.
    Vice-Chancellor Boylston Green
UNIVERSITY OF VIRGINIA, Charlottesville, Va.
    Professor A. G. A. Balz
VANDERBILT UNIVERSITY, Nashville, Tenn.
    Dr. W. C. Curry
WASHINGTON AND LEE UNIVERSITY, Lexington, Va.
    Dean James G. Leyburn

# CONSITITUTION

### Article I. Name and Object

The name of the organization shall be the Southern Humanities Conference.

The object of the Conference shall be the advancement in the South, of teaching and research in the Humanities, and the maintenance and strengthening of relations among Southern societies devoted to such purposes.

### Article II. Members

1. The members of the Conference shall be:
   a. one member appointed by each constituent organization, who shall serve as its delegate in the Conference;
   b. four members-at-large, or a number equal to one-third the number of constituent organizations, whichever is the larger, elected by the Conference;
   c. one or more representatives of the American Council of Learned Societies, as chosen by that organization;
   d. officers of the Conference, who may, or may not, be delegates or members-at-large.

2. Members of the Conference shall be appointed or elected as follows:
   a. members appointed by constituent organizations shall be chosen in such manner as the several organizations may respectively determine;
   b. members-at-large shall be elected in the annual meeting from a list of names prepared by the Executive Committee. This Committee shall prepare a list which shall contain at least twice as many names as the number

of members-at-large to be elected; this list shall be communicated to all Conference members forty-five days in advance of the annual meeting. At the same time the Executive Committee shall invite suggestions from the members. The Executive Committee shall prepare, and shall present at the annual meeting of the Conference, a final list in which they shall incorporate and so designate any nominations proposed by two or more members which shall have been communicated to the Executive Committee fifteen days in advance of the annual meeting;

c. members of the Executive Committee shall be elected at the annual meeting from a list of names prepared by a Nominating Committee. The Nominating Committee shall prepare a list which shall contain at least twice as many names as the number of members to be elected, selected from among the members of the Conference with due regard to regional, institutional, and disciplinary distribution; this list shall be communicated to all Conference members forty-five days in advance of the annual meeting. At the same time the Nominating Committee shall invite suggestions from the members of the Conference. The Nominating Committee shall prepare, and shall present at the annual meeting of the Conference, a final list in which they shall incorporate and so designate any nominations proposed by two or more members which shall have been communicated to the Nominating Committee fifteen days in advance of the annual meeting.

3. a. The terms of all delegates and members-at-large shall be three years, arranged in such rotation that approximately

one third of the terms shall expire on December 31 of each year.

b. Members-at-large having served one term of three years shall not be eligible for immediate re-appointment or re-election as members-at-large.

c. The place of any member which shall be vacated before the expiration of his term shall be filled only for the remainder of the term; the place of any member-at-large so vacated shall be filled by appointment by the Executive Committee.

*Article III. Constituent Organizations*

1. The constituent organizations of the Conference shall be the following:

   American Musicological Society, Southeastern Chapter
   Classical Association of the Middle West and South, Southern Section
   College Art Association, Southeastern Conference
   Society of Biblical Literature and Exegesis, Southern Section
   South Atlantic Modern Language Association
   South-Central Modern Language Association
   Southeastern Library Association
   Southern Historical Association
   Southern Society for the Philosophy of Religion
   Southern Society for Philosophy and Psychology
   and, also, any other regional Southern organization devoted to humanistic studies which may be admitted to representation in the Conference by a vote of three-fourths of all members.

2. Any constituent organization which at any annual meeting of the Conference shall announce its intention to terminate

its representation in the Conference may at the succeeding annual meeting effect such termination, whereupon the membership of its delegate in the Conference shall cease.

3. A constituent organization may be excluded from representation in the Conference, for sufficient reason, by a vote of three-fourths of all the members of the Conference.

## Article IV. Officers

1. The officers of the Conference shall be a Chairman and a Secretary-Treasurer, who shall not serve for more than three successive years.

2. The Nominating Committee shall communicate to the members of the Conference, forty-five days before the annual meeting, nominations for the officers of the Conference. The Nominating Committee shall prepare and communicate to the members of the Conference, fifteen days in advance of the annual meeting, a final list in which shall be included, together with its own nominations, all names that have been prepared by two or more members of the Conference.

3. The Chairman shall preside at the meetings of the Conference and shall otherwise perform the duties of Chairman of the Conference. The Secretary-Treasurer shall perform the usual duties of these offices, as instructed by the Executive Committee.

## Article V. Nominating Committee

The Chairman shall appoint each year a Nominating Committee of three members of the Conference. The Committee shall prepare a list of nominations for Conference officers, and shall make any other nominations requested by the Conference or the Executive Committee.

## Article VI. Executive Committee

There shall be an Executive Committee which shall consist of three members, elected by the Conference as provided in Article II, 2, and also of the Chairman, and Secretary-Treasurer, *ex officiis*. The three elected members of the Committee shall serve terms of three years, commencing at the close of the annual meeting in which they have been elected, in such rotation that the term of one member of the Committee shall expire each year.

## Article VII. Meetings

1. The Conference shall hold an annual meeting at such time and place as it may determine, for the election of officers, members-at-large, and members of the Executive Committee; for the approval of the budget; for the consideration of reports and recommendations from the Executive Committee; for the formation of policies, and of instructions to the Executive Committee; and for the transaction of such other business as may come before it.

2. In any meeting of the Conference a majority of all the members of the Conference shall be a quorum requisite for the transaction of business.

3. Each member in attendance at any meeting of the Conference shall be entitled to one vote upon all matters requiring action by the Conference.

## Article VIII. Various

1. The Conference shall adopt such regulations and rules as may be necessary to give full effect to this Constitution and to determine its procedure.

2. Amendments to this Constitution may be adopted in any duly called meeting of the Conference by vote of two-thirds

of the members present, notice of such proposed amendments having been communicated to the members of the Council forty-five days in advance of the meeting, and shall take effect when ratified by a majority of the constituent organizations.

3. The Conference may be permanently dissolved only at a special meeting called for the purpose by vote of three-fourths of all its members.

www.ingramcontent.com/pod-product-compliance
Lightning Source LLC
Chambersburg PA
CBHW031714230426
43668CB00006B/214